Maximilian]

The Saint Who Defied Hate With Love

©

BENEDICT DELAROSA

Introduction: Why Kolbe's Story Matters Today....... 8
   Kolbe's Relevance in a Fractured World................ 10
   Kolbe's Journey: Faith and Action......................... 12
   A Life of Courage Under Oppression..................... 14
   The Goals of This Biography................................. 16
   How This Biography Stands Out............................ 18
   A Legacy for Today and Tomorrow....................... 20

Chapter 1: The Boy Who Dreamed of the Immaculate..22
   A Humble Beginning... 23
   A Child of Curiosity and Devotion........................ 25
   A Vision That Changed Everything....................... 27
   The Seeds of a Mission.. 29
   Cultural and Religious Influences in Zduńska Wola... 30
   The Role of Family in His Spiritual Formation....... 31
   A Glimpse of What Was to Come.......................... 33

Chapter 2: A Journey into Faith............................. 36
   The Call to Religious Life..................................... 37
   Joining the Conventual Franciscans...................... 39
   Years in Rome: A Scholar's Pilgrimage................. 41
   Faith Meets Reason... 42
   The Birth of the Militia Immaculatae.................... 44
   Challenges and Growth... 46
   A Visionary's Foundation..................................... 47

Chapter 3: Militia Immaculatae: The Army of the Immaculate..50

    The Birth of the Militia Immaculatae......................52
    The Early Efforts.. 55
    A Movement Gains Momentum............................57
    Inspiring the Laity..59
    Facing Opposition..61
    A Legacy Begins..62
Chapter 4: The Publisher of Faith............................. 64
    A Bold Venture in Faith... 65
    A Magazine with a Mission..................................... 66
    Innovative Methods in Catholic Media................... 69
    Stories that Transformed Lives................................ 71
    Overcoming Challenges...72
    A Global Impact.. 74
    Conversations and Inspirations................................ 75
    Building Toward a Legacy.......................................76
Chapter 5: Expanding the Mission............................. 78
    The Birth of Niepokalanów: "City of the
    Immaculate"..78
    Building from Scratch..79
    Niepokalanów's Spiritual Vibrancy......................... 82
    A Missionary's Call to Japan...................................83
    Founding the Garden of the Immaculate................. 85
    Challenges and Triumphs in Japan.......................... 87
    A Growing Influence... 88
    Dialogues of Faith..89
    Legacy of the Mission in Japan............................... 91
    Back to Poland: Expanding the Vision.................... 92

    Setting the Stage for Greater Sacrifices...................93
Chapter 6: Under Nazi Occupation............................ 94
    The Storm of War Descends.................................. 94
    The Nazi Occupation and Its Impact....................... 95
    Sheltering Refugees: Acts of Defiance...................97
    Resistance Through Faith.. 99
    Facing Nazi Persecution.. 100
    Sacrifices for the Greater Good............................. 102
    Witnessing to Faith Amid Darkness...................... 103
    Preparing for the Ultimate Sacrifice...................... 104
    Legacy of Courage...105
Chapter 7: A Witness to Hope in Auschwitz............ 107
    Arrest and Imprisonment....................................... 107
    Arrival at Auschwitz..109
    A Light in the Darkness.. 110
    The Ultimate Test of Love..................................... 112
    The Starvation Bunker.. 115
    Final Days... 116
    The Life Saved..117
    A Legacy of Hope...118
Chapter 8: Echoes of Heroism: Survivors'
Testimonies.. 119
    A Light in the Darkness.. 119
    Franciszek Gajowniczek's Testimony................... 121
    Other Survivors Speak.. 123
    Kolbe's Legacy of Resilience................................ 125
    Kolbe's Impact Beyond Auschwitz....................... 126

A Message for All Generations........................... 128
Auschwitz as Sacred Ground............................... 129
A Legacy That Lives On.. 130
A Death That Reverberated Beyond Auschwitz.... 131
The Initial Steps Toward Recognition................... 133
Testimonies of Miracles.. 135
Beatification by Pope Paul VI............................... 136
Pope John Paul II and the Canonization Process... 138
Declared a Martyr of Charity................................ 140
Kolbe's Influence on the Modern World............... 141
The Legacy of a Saint.. 143
Dialogue and Reflection.. 144
A Saint for the Modern World............................... 145
Patron Saint of Our Times..................................... 146
Pro-Life Advocacy: A Testament to the Sanctity of Life..149
Addiction Recovery: A Journey of Hope............... 151
Modern Marian Devotion: The Army of the Immaculate... 153
Inspiring Resilience in Modern Challenges.......... 155
Dialogues that Echo Through Generations........... 156
A Saint for All.. 157

Chapter 11: The Mystical Depths of Kolbe's Teachings.. 159
The Theology of Suffering and Redemptive Love 161
A Love That Redeems... 163
Kolbe's Unique Devotion to the Immaculate

Conception.. 165
The Immaculate Conception and Catholic Theology.. 167
Dialogues that Illuminate His Teachings............... 169
A Legacy of Mystical Depth................................171

Chapter 12: Kolbe and the Science of Faith............173
The Scholar with a Scientific Mind....................... 174
Integrating Science into Faith............................... 176
A Model for Bridging Faith and Reason............... 178
Dialogues and Intellectual Encounters.................. 180
Kolbe's Philosophical Contributions..................... 182
Faith and Science in Modern Contexts.................. 184
A Vision for Intellectual Spirituality..................... 185

Conclusion: Living the Kolbe Legacy – Defying Hate with Love in Today's World..188
Living the Kolbe Legacy: Lessons from His Life. 189
Kolbe's Relevance in Today's World.....................191
A Call to Selflessness... 193
Faith as a Catalyst for Change............................... 194
Defying Hate with Love... 196
A Legacy of Hope and Action............................... 197
A Call to Action...199
A Final Reflection..201

Appendices...203
Timeline of Saint Maximilian Kolbe's Life...........203
Selected Writings of Saint Maximilian Kolbe....... 206
Prayers Inspired by Saint Maximilian Kolbe.........208

    A Prayer for Courage and Love 208
    A Prayer for Marian Devotion 208
    A Prayer for Perseverance in Faith 209
References 210
   Primary Sources 210
   Biographies and Scholarly Works 211
   Historical Context 212
   Documentaries 213

Copyright © BENEDICT DELAROSA (2024) All rights reserved. No part of this publication may be reproduced, distributed, or transmitted in any form or by any means, including photocopying, recording, or other electronic or mechanical methods, without the prior written permission of the publisher, except in the case of brief quotations embodied in critical reviews and certain other noncommercial uses permitted by copyright law.

Introduction: Why Kolbe's Story Matters Today

In a dark, suffocating cell in Auschwitz—a place synonymous with unspeakable cruelty and despair—a man knelt in prayer. His skeletal frame bore the marks of starvation and suffering, yet his eyes radiated peace. Around him, other prisoners—equally ravaged by hunger—drew strength from his presence. Maximilian Kolbe, a Catholic priest, had willingly taken the place of another man condemned to die. As the days in the starvation bunker dragged on, Kolbe transformed the space into a sanctuary of hope. His prayers and hymns echoed through the corridors of death, a testament to the unyielding power of faith and love in the face of unimaginable hate.

Kolbe's final act of selflessness—offering his life to save Franciszek Gajowniczek, a stranger—was more than just an individual sacrifice. It was a profound statement of defiance against the dehumanizing forces of Nazi ideology. In a world where life had been stripped of dignity and reduced to a number, Kolbe's choice affirmed the sanctity of every human soul. His death was not merely a martyrdom; it was a triumph of love over hate, of faith over despair, and of selflessness over self-preservation.

Kolbe's Relevance in a Fractured World

Maximilian Kolbe's story is not just a relic of the past; it is a beacon for today's world, where division, hatred, and indifference often dominate headlines. His life challenges us to confront modern injustices with the same courage and love that defined his existence.

Consider the parallels: Kolbe's era was marked by oppressive regimes, ideological extremism, and widespread suffering. Today, we grapple with our own forms of division—racial injustice, religious persecution, political polarization, and a rising tide of apathy toward human suffering. Kolbe's unwavering faith and willingness to stand up for others remind us that love is not passive; it demands action, often at great personal cost.

Kolbe's sacrifice also speaks powerfully to the value of forgiveness. In a world that often glorifies vengeance, his ability to respond to hatred with compassion is a radical, transformative example. His life inspires us to resist the temptation to repay harm with harm and instead choose a path of healing and reconciliation.

Kolbe's Journey: Faith and Action

To understand Kolbe's extraordinary martyrdom, we must first delve into his life—a journey defined by unwavering devotion, intellectual brilliance, and a relentless drive to serve others. From his humble beginnings in Zduńska Wola, Poland, to his theological studies in Rome, and eventually to his founding of the Niepokalanów monastery and Militia Immaculatae (Army of the Immaculate),

Kolbe's life was a testament to the power of faith in action.

His decision to join the Conventual Franciscans was not merely a personal calling but a response to a vision he believed was divinely inspired. As a boy, he experienced a Marian apparition that shaped the course of his life, setting him on a mission to spread devotion to the Virgin Mary as a means of combating indifference and atheism.

Kolbe's innovative use of media—through the publication of *Knight of the Immaculate* magazine—demonstrates his forward-thinking approach to evangelization. He understood that the

Gospel needed to meet people where they were, and his efforts to make Catholic teachings accessible and engaging were revolutionary for his time.

A Life of Courage Under Oppression

Kolbe's story takes on a new dimension during World War II, when Poland fell under Nazi occupation. As the Nazis sought to extinguish religious and cultural identity, Kolbe stood firm in his convictions. His monastery, Nicpokalanów, became a refuge for thousands of displaced people, including Jews fleeing persecution. Despite repeated arrests and brutal treatment,

Kolbe remained steadfast, using every opportunity to minister to the suffering and marginalized.

His arrest in 1941 marked the beginning of his final chapter. In Auschwitz, Kolbe's faith became a source of strength not just for himself but for all those around him. In a place designed to break the human spirit, he offered hope. His decision to take the place of Franciszek Gajowniczek—a husband and father who begged for his life—was the ultimate act of self-giving love.

The Goals of This Biography

This book seeks to tell Kolbe's story in its entirety, capturing the man behind the saint. While many accounts focus on his martyrdom, this biography aims to provide a fuller picture of his life: his intellectual pursuits, his visionary leadership, his theological insights, and his enduring legacy.

In particular, this book will address aspects of Kolbe's life often overlooked in other biographies. His integration of science and faith, his Marian theology, and his innovative approaches to evangelization deserve deeper exploration. By delving into these facets, we hope to present Kolbe not only as a martyr but as a visionary leader whose teachings remain relevant today.

Moreover, this biography aims to inspire readers to apply Kolbe's principles in their own lives. Whether confronting personal struggles, standing against injustice, or seeking to deepen their faith, readers will find in Kolbe a guide and companion for their journey.

How This Biography Stands Out

Unlike many existing accounts, this book takes a holistic approach, weaving together Kolbe's personal, intellectual, and spiritual dimensions.

Each chapter is carefully crafted to immerse readers in his world, using vivid descriptions, firsthand accounts, and historical context.

For instance, instead of merely recounting Kolbe's vision of the Virgin Mary, we explore its psychological and spiritual impact on a young boy growing up in early 20th-century Poland. Similarly, when discussing his work in Japan, we delve into the cultural and religious challenges he faced, highlighting his adaptability and resilience.

The book also incorporates survivor testimonies and lesser-known writings by Kolbe, offering fresh insights into his character and teachings. By drawing on a wide range of sources, this biography ensures a nuanced and authentic portrayal of Kolbe's life.

A Legacy for Today and Tomorrow

Kolbe's story is not confined to history books or religious circles. It resonates across cultures and generations, offering timeless lessons on the power of love, the importance of faith, and the courage to stand up for what is right.

As we navigate a world rife with challenges, Kolbe's example reminds us that even in the darkest times, light can shine through acts of compassion and selflessness. His life is a testament to the transformative power of love—a love that defies hate, bridges divides, and inspires hope.

This biography is an invitation to walk with Kolbe, to see the world through his eyes, and to embrace his vision of a world transformed by the Immaculate's love. It is a call to action for all who seek to live with purpose, courage, and grace.

Chapter 1: The Boy Who Dreamed of the Immaculate

In the heart of Zduńska Wola, a modest town in central Poland, the cobbled streets echoed with the rhythms of a community deeply rooted in faith and tradition. At the turn of the 20th century, Zduńska Wola was a place where life moved at an unhurried pace, yet its people bore the weight of national struggles. Poland was a country partitioned by powerful empires—Russia, Prussia, and Austria—and its people clung fiercely to their Catholic faith as both a spiritual anchor and a symbol of national identity. Here, amidst simple homes and small workshops, a boy named Rajmund Kolbe would take his first steps on a path that would lead to sainthood.

A Humble Beginning

Rajmund Kolbe was born on January 8, 1894, into a family that mirrored the resilience and faith of their town. His parents, Juliusz and Marianna Kolbe, were hardworking and devout Catholics who instilled in their children a deep love for God. Juliusz worked as a weaver, while Marianna managed the household, raising Rajmund and his siblings in an environment where prayer and service were integral to daily life.

The Kolbe household was modest but filled with warmth. Despite financial struggles, Juliusz and Marianna prioritized their children's education and spiritual growth. They taught them the value of sacrifice, often reminding them that their faith was the greatest inheritance they could pass on. Rajmund's upbringing was steeped in the rituals of Catholic life—daily prayers, Sunday Mass, and Marian devotions were not mere traditions but lifelines that connected the family to their Creator.

Yet life was not without its hardships. The Kolbe family faced periods of extreme poverty, often surviving on little more than potatoes and bread. Juliusz's work as a weaver was unstable, and there were times when the family had to rely on the charity of neighbors. Despite these challenges, Marianna's unwavering faith and resilience became a source of inspiration for young Rajmund.

A Child of Curiosity and Devotion

From a young age, Rajmund exhibited a blend of traits that set him apart: an insatiable curiosity and a remarkable sensitivity to spiritual matters. He was an inquisitive child, often found pondering questions about the universe, God, and the meaning of life. His parents noted his precociousness and encouraged him to channel his energy into both study and prayer.

Rajmund's fascination with the Virgin Mary emerged early. Marianna, who had a particular devotion to the Immaculate Conception, would often speak to her children about Mary's purity and role as the Mother of God. These stories planted seeds in Rajmund's heart, nurturing a love for the Blessed Mother that would only grow deeper with time.

A Vision That Changed Everything

In 1906, at the tender age of 12, Rajmund experienced an event that would forever alter the trajectory of his life. Troubled by his own youthful restlessness and the fear of falling short of God's expectations, he turned to prayer, seeking guidance. One day, while kneeling in the small, dimly lit family chapel, he had a profound vision.

As Rajmund later recounted, the Virgin Mary appeared to him holding two crowns: one white and one red. The white crown symbolized purity, and the red represented martyrdom. Mary asked him, "Which do you choose?"

In awe of her presence, Rajmund hesitated for only a moment before responding, "I choose both."

This vision was more than a mystical experience; it was a call to a life of extraordinary devotion and sacrifice. The encounter left him with a deep sense of mission and purpose, shaping his understanding of what it meant to live a holy life. The two crowns would become enduring symbols of his journey, representing his commitment to both spiritual purity and the ultimate sacrifice of his life.

The Seeds of a Mission

The vision ignited a fire within Rajmund. He began to dedicate himself to prayer and study with renewed fervor. His classmates noticed the change, often teasing him for his piety, but Rajmund remained undeterred. He saw his life as belonging entirely to God, and this conviction became the lens through which he viewed the world.

Marianna, sensing the profound transformation in her son, encouraged him to embrace his calling. She later admitted that while she was proud of Rajmund's spiritual growth, it came with a bittersweet realization that he was destined for a path that might lead him far from home—and possibly to great suffering.

Cultural and Religious Influences in Zduńska Wola

The town of Zduńska Wola played a significant role in shaping Rajmund's faith. Its close-knit Catholic community offered a tapestry of traditions that fostered devotion. The parish church, with its towering steeple and vibrant stained glass, was the heart of the town. It was here that Rajmund learned the power of liturgy and the beauty of communal worship.

The political climate of the time also left its mark. Living under foreign rule, the people of Poland often found solace in their faith. For young Rajmund, the intersection of religion and national identity became a source of inspiration. He saw in Mary not just the Mother of God but a protector of the Polish people, a figure who embodied hope and resilience.

The Role of Family in His Spiritual Formation

Juliusz and Marianna's influence on Rajmund cannot be overstated. Their unwavering commitment to their faith served as a model for their children. Juliusz, though often preoccupied with work, made time for prayer and reflection, teaching Rajmund the importance of balancing labor with spiritual devotion.

Marianna's role was even more profound. Her own life was marked by sacrifice and an abiding trust in God's providence. She would often remind her children that true happiness came not from material wealth but from living in accordance with God's will. For Rajmund, these lessons became the foundation of his vocation.

A Glimpse of What Was to Come

As Rajmund grew older, the vision of the two crowns remained vivid in his mind. It guided his decisions and fueled his desire to serve God in a unique and powerful way. Though he was still a boy, those who knew him sensed that he was destined for something extraordinary.

His childhood in Zduńska Wola was not merely a prelude to his later life but a crucible in which his character and faith were forged. The struggles he faced, the lessons he learned, and the experiences he had all contributed to the formation of a young man who would one day change the world.

Rajmund Kolbe's early years were marked by a blend of simplicity and spiritual depth. In the modest surroundings of Zduńska Wola, he developed a faith that was both childlike in its purity and profound in its intensity. The Marian vision he experienced as a boy set him on a path of extraordinary devotion, laying the groundwork for a life defined by love, sacrifice, and unwavering faith.

As we journey deeper into Kolbe's story, we will see how these formative years shaped the man who would one day stand as a beacon of hope in one of history's darkest hours. His childhood was not merely a beginning but a testament to the power of grace at work in the lives of those who open their hearts to God.

Chapter 2: A Journey into Faith

The decision to dedicate one's life to God is rarely a straightforward path, and for Rajmund Kolbe, the journey into the Conventual Franciscans was both deeply personal and divinely guided. By the time he reached adolescence, the vision of the Virgin Mary offering him two crowns—one of purity and one of martyrdom—was etched indelibly into his soul. That moment had ignited a fire within him, and while his devotion to Mary and his faith grew stronger, the world around him began to call him to a life of service and sacrifice.

The Call to Religious Life

In his early teenage years, Rajmund displayed a profound maturity and spiritual awareness that set him apart. While other boys his age were consumed by the joys of youthful pursuits, Rajmund was drawn to prayer, reflection, and study. His parents, Juliusz and Marianna, watched with a mixture of pride and trepidation as their son's devotion to God deepened.

One evening, Rajmund approached his mother as she knelt by her bedside in prayer. "Mama," he began hesitantly, "do you think I could ever do enough to repay the love of Jesus and Mary?"

Marianna looked up at her son, her eyes filled with both tenderness and a mother's quiet resignation. "My son," she said softly, "you don't need to repay their love. You only need to accept it fully and let it guide your life."

These words seemed to crystallize something in Rajmund's heart. Soon after, he confided to his parents his desire to join the Conventual Franciscans. It was a decision that filled them with mixed emotions—pride in his calling and sadness at the prospect of his leaving home. Marianna, ever the pillar of faith, offered him her blessing, saying, "If this is God's will for you, then it is also mine."

Joining the Conventual Franciscans

At the age of 13, Rajmund left his family and entered the junior seminary of the Conventual Franciscans in Lwów (now Lviv, Ukraine). It was a difficult transition for the young boy, who had never been far from the comforts of home. The seminary's austere environment, with its rigorous schedule of prayer, study, and manual labor, was both challenging and transformative.

Rajmund quickly earned a reputation among his peers for his intelligence, humility, and unwavering devotion. One of his classmates later recalled, "Even as a boy, Rajmund seemed to carry a quiet strength, as if he were always in the presence of something greater than himself."

But seminary life was not without its struggles. Rajmund faced moments of homesickness and self-doubt, questioning whether he was truly worthy of the calling he had embraced. During one particularly difficult period, he confided in his spiritual director, who encouraged him to persevere. "Remember," the priest said, "it is not perfection that God seeks, but a heart willing to follow Him."

Years in Rome: A Scholar's Pilgrimage

In 1912, Rajmund, now Brother Maximilian, was sent to Rome to continue his studies at the Pontifical Gregorian University and later at the International Seraphic College. These years in the Eternal City were transformative, offering him not only rigorous academic training but also a broader perspective on the Church's universal mission.

Rome was a bustling center of intellectual and spiritual life, and Maximilian immersed himself in its vibrant culture. He excelled in his studies, earning doctorates in both philosophy and theology. Yet, his academic achievements were not ends in themselves; they were tools for a greater purpose. Maximilian believed that the pursuit of knowledge was a means to glorify God and to better serve humanity.

Faith Meets Reason

Maximilian's time in Rome exposed him to the challenges of modernity. He encountered new philosophical movements, some of which sought to undermine the Church's teachings. The rise of secularism and atheism troubled him deeply, but it also fueled his determination to defend the faith through reasoned argument and evangelization.

One evening, during a lively debate with fellow seminarians, Maximilian articulated his vision with characteristic passion. "The truth of God," he argued, "is not opposed to reason. On the contrary, faith and reason are like two wings that lift the soul to the heights of understanding."

This commitment to bridging faith and reason became a cornerstone of Maximilian's mission. He saw the intellectual battleground of his time as an opportunity to engage with the world rather than retreat from it.

The Birth of the Militia Immaculatae

It was during these years in Rome that Maximilian had a pivotal encounter that would shape his life's work. While walking through the city's streets one afternoon, he witnessed an anti-Catholic demonstration led by members of the Freemasons. They marched boldly through St. Peter's Square, carrying banners that blasphemed the Virgin Mary and the Church.

The sight filled Maximilian with righteous indignation and a sense of urgency. He later wrote in his journal, "The enemies of the Church are bold in their efforts.

How much more bold must we be in defending her and spreading the love of the Immaculate!"

In response, Maximilian founded the Militia Immaculatae (Army of the Immaculate) in 1917, a movement dedicated to promoting Marian devotion and combating indifference to God. The Militia's mission was clear: to bring the world closer to Christ through the intercession of Mary. Its motto, "To Jesus through Mary," encapsulated Maximilian's belief in Mary as the surest path to holiness.

Challenges and Growth

Maximilian's fervor and vision were not without challenges. His health, already fragile due to tuberculosis, often left him physically weakened. Yet, he refused to let illness deter him from his mission. "Suffering," he once said, "is a gift that allows us to unite ourselves more closely with Christ."

His fellow Franciscans were inspired by his unwavering determination. Brother Pio, one of his closest companions, recalled, "Maximilian had a way of making you believe that no obstacle was insurmountable. His faith was contagious, and his devotion to Mary was unshakeable."

A Visionary's Foundation

By the time Maximilian completed his studies and was ordained a priest in 1918, he had laid the groundwork for a mission that would span continents and touch countless lives. His intellectual pursuits in Rome had deepened his understanding of the faith, while his encounters with the challenges of modernity had strengthened his resolve to bring Christ to the world.

Maximilian returned to Poland not as a young boy with dreams of the Immaculate, but as a man armed with the conviction and tools to make those dreams a reality. His journey into faith was far from complete, but it had set the stage for the extraordinary work that lay ahead.

In all, Maximilian Kolbe's journey into faith was a tapestry woven with moments of struggle, revelation, and triumph. From his decision to join the Conventual Franciscans to his years of rigorous study in Rome, each step was marked by a deepening of his devotion to God and his commitment to serving others. His ability to merge faith with reason, to confront challenges with courage, and to inspire others with his vision made him not just a man of faith, but a leader whose influence would transcend his time.

As we turn to the next chapter, we will see how Maximilian's dreams of spreading devotion to the Immaculate began to take tangible form. His journey into faith was not merely personal; it was the foundation of a mission that would transform lives and leave an indelible mark on the Church and the world.

Chapter 3: Militia Immaculatae: The Army of the Immaculate

In the fall of 1917, the streets of Rome were alive with tension. The Great War was tearing through Europe, leaving devastation in its wake, and ideological movements were rising in defiance of the Church. It was during this tumultuous time that Maximilian Kolbe, still a young friar studying in Rome, experienced a moment of clarity that would shape the rest of his life.

The spark came one afternoon as he walked through St. Peter's Square. A loud procession of Freemasons disrupted the serene atmosphere of the Vatican. They marched with banners depicting Satan crushing St. Michael the Archangel and distributed pamphlets attacking the Church. "The enemy is not hiding," Maximilian muttered to himself, his hands clenched. "They march openly, proud of their rebellion."

Maximilian felt a surge of righteous indignation. It wasn't anger that consumed him, but a deep sadness for the lost souls and a burning desire to counteract the darkness spreading in the world. He returned to his small room in the seminary and spent the evening in prayer, seeking guidance. He wrote later in his journal, "How can we stand idly by when the enemies of the Church work so tirelessly? Should we not be just as bold in proclaiming the truth of Christ and the love of Mary?"

The Birth of the Militia Immaculatae

The answer came in the form of a vision. As Maximilian knelt in prayer before a statue of the Blessed Virgin Mary, an idea began to crystallize in his mind: an army of laypeople and religious dedicated to spreading devotion to the Immaculate Virgin as a means to bring souls closer to Christ.

This would be no ordinary movement. It would be a spiritual militia, united under the banner of the Immaculate Conception, to combat the forces of indifference and atheism.

In October 1917, Maximilian gathered six of his fellow friars in a modest room at the International Seraphic College. "We must act," he began, his voice steady but passionate. "Our Blessed Mother, the Immaculate, has been given to us as a refuge and a guide. Through her, we can conquer hearts for Christ. But we cannot do this alone. We must form an army—not of violence, but of love and devotion."

The friars listened intently as Maximilian outlined his vision. They would call the movement the *Militia Immaculatae*—the Army of the Immaculate. Its mission was simple yet profound: to bring the world closer to Christ through Mary. Members would consecrate themselves to the Immaculate Virgin, wear her Miraculous Medal as a sign of their commitment, and dedicate their lives to prayer, penance, and evangelization.

One of the friars, Brother Louis, voiced a concern. "But how will we reach people, Brother Maximilian? We are just a handful of friars with no resources."

Maximilian smiled. "The Immaculate will provide," he said confidently. "This is her work, not ours. All we need to do is trust her completely and give her everything we have."

The Early Efforts

The first steps of the *Militia Immaculatae* were small but significant. Maximilian and his companions began by spreading the message within their seminary and among nearby parishes. They distributed Miraculous Medals and explained their significance to anyone who would listen.

To deepen the spiritual foundation of the movement, Maximilian wrote a simple but profound prayer of consecration to the Immaculate Virgin:

"O Immaculate Virgin, Queen of Heaven and Earth, refuge of sinners and our most loving Mother, God has willed to entrust the entire order of mercy to you. I, [name], a repentant sinner, cast myself at your feet, humbly imploring you to take me with all that I am and have, wholly to yourself as your possession and property."

This prayer would become the cornerstone of the *Militia Immaculatae's* mission, inspiring countless souls to place their lives under Mary's protection.

A Movement Gains Momentum

By the time Maximilian returned to Poland in 1919, the *Militia Immaculatae* was beginning to gain traction. The aftermath of World War I left many people searching for hope and meaning, and Maximilian's message of Marian devotion resonated deeply. He traveled tirelessly, speaking at parishes, organizing prayer groups, and encouraging people to join the movement.

One memorable encounter occurred in a small village outside Warsaw. After giving a stirring homily on the power of Mary's intercession, a woman approached Maximilian with tears in her eyes. "Father," she said, clutching a Miraculous Medal, "I have been so lost, so hopeless. But today, you've given me a reason to believe again. I want to join your army."

Maximilian placed a hand on her shoulder and said gently, "The Immaculate never abandons her children. She has called you today, and she will guide you every step of the way."

Inspiring the Laity

One of Maximilian's greatest gifts was his ability to inspire ordinary people to become extraordinary instruments of God's love. He believed that everyone, regardless of their state in life, could contribute to the mission of the Church.

"Every soul is a battlefield," he often said. "But with Mary, we can conquer even the hardest hearts."

This belief led him to emphasize the role of laypeople in the *Militia Immaculatae.* He encouraged them to see their daily lives as opportunities for evangelization, whether through simple acts of kindness, sharing their faith with others, or praying for the conversion of sinners.

Maximilian also understood the power of media in spreading the movement's message. In 1922, he founded a magazine called *Rycerz Niepokalanej (Knight of the Immaculate)*, which quickly became a powerful tool for evangelization. Through its pages, he shared stories of faith, teachings on Marian devotion, and updates on the work of the *Militia Immaculatae*.

Facing Opposition

As the *Militia Immaculatae* grew, so did the challenges. Maximilian faced criticism from those who viewed his devotion to Mary as excessive or misguided. Some even accused him of promoting superstition.

But Maximilian remained undeterred. "Love for the Immaculate," he once said, "is not an obstacle to loving Christ. It is the surest path to Him."

He also encountered logistical obstacles, from limited resources to political tensions. Yet, he never allowed these difficulties to dampen his resolve. Whenever the work seemed impossible, Maximilian turned to

Mary in prayer, trusting that she would open the necessary doors.

A Legacy Begins

By the late 1920s, the *Militia Immaculatae* had grown into a global movement, with tens of thousands of members across Europe and beyond. What had begun as a small gathering of friars in Rome had become a powerful force for good, drawing people closer to Christ through the intercession of Mary.

Maximilian's vision for the *Militia Immaculatae* was not just about numbers; it was about transforming hearts and renewing the world.

He believed that through Mary's intercession, even the most hardened souls could experience the love and mercy of God.

As we move to the next chapter, we will see how Maximilian's passion for evangelization and his innovative use of media propelled the *Militia Immaculatae* to new heights, solidifying its place as one of the most influential Catholic movements of the 20th century.

Chapter 4: The Publisher of Faith

In the quiet Polish town of Grodno in 1922, Maximilian Kolbe's vision for the *Militia Immaculatae* took a groundbreaking turn. While the spiritual movement had already begun gathering momentum, Kolbe saw an untapped opportunity: the power of the written word to reach hearts and minds. He realized that while sermons and personal evangelization were effective, they were limited in scope. But a magazine—produced with care, passion, and purpose—could transcend borders and reach tens of thousands. Thus, *the Knight of the Immaculate* was born.

A Bold Venture in Faith

When Kolbe first proposed creating a Catholic magazine, skepticism abounded. He lacked the funds, the resources, and even the proper equipment. "How do you plan to start a publication without so much as a printing press?" one of his confreres asked, raising an eyebrow.

Kolbe's response was characteristically calm but resolute. "The Immaculate will provide," he said simply, his eyes reflecting unshakable faith.

The initial setup was humble. Kolbe, along with a few dedicated friars, began the work of publishing the magazine in a small room at their friary. They worked tirelessly, often late into the night, writing, editing, and assembling content. The first issue of *Rycerz Niepokalanej* (*Knight of the Immaculate*) rolled off the press in January 1922, with a print run of just 5,000 copies.

A Magazine with a Mission

From the very beginning, Kolbe envisioned *Knight of the Immaculate* as more than just a magazine; it was a tool for evangelization. Its content was carefully curated to inspire devotion to the Blessed Virgin Mary and to combat the growing secularism and atheism of the time.

Each issue included a mix of articles:

- Stories of Marian apparitions and miracles, written to ignite faith and wonder in readers.

- Practical advice on how to live a life of holiness in the modern world.

- Thought-provoking reflections on theology, science, and faith, showcasing Kolbe's belief in the harmony between reason and religion.

- Updates on the activities of the *Militia Immaculatae* to encourage readers to join and participate actively.

One of the early articles written by Kolbe himself bore the title "*Mary: The Shortcut to Christ.*" In it, he wrote, "The Immaculate is not a detour but the quickest and most direct route to Jesus. To love her is to love Him more perfectly."

Readers were captivated. Letters began pouring in from all over Poland, praising the magazine for its engaging content and spiritual depth. "Father Maximilian," one letter read, "your magazine has brought light into my home. My family reads it together every evening, and it has strengthened our faith."

Innovative Methods in Catholic Media

Kolbe was not content to rely on traditional methods of distribution. He was a visionary, constantly seeking new ways to reach a broader audience. He encouraged friars and lay volunteers to personally distribute the magazine in towns and villages. Some walked for miles, carrying stacks of the *Knight of the Immaculate* in their arms, eager to share its message.

But Kolbe's ambition didn't stop at Poland's borders. Recognizing the need for Catholic media on a global scale, he began translating the magazine into other languages, including Italian and Japanese.

He envisioned a day when the *Knight of the Immaculate* would be read in every corner of the world.

To achieve this, he invested in improving the friary's printing facilities. With donations from benefactors and his own resourcefulness, Kolbe acquired more advanced printing presses. By the late 1920s, the print run of the magazine had grown to over 70,000 copies per issue—a staggering number for a religious publication at the time.

Stories that Transformed Lives

The power of the *Knight of the Immaculate* lay in its ability to touch souls in profound ways. One remarkable story involves a man named Jan, a factory worker in Kraków. Disillusioned by the harsh realities of his life, Jan had drifted away from the Church. One day, he picked up a copy of the magazine at a friend's house.

"Mary will never abandon you," the article said, echoing Kolbe's unwavering trust in the Virgin.

Those words struck a chord in Jan's heart. He began attending Mass again and eventually joined the *Militia Immaculatae*. Years later, he would recount his story to Kolbe himself, saying, "Father, your magazine saved me. It reminded me that I was never alone, even in my darkest moments."

Such testimonies were not uncommon. The magazine's blend of spiritual guidance, practical wisdom, and uplifting stories made it a beacon of hope for countless readers.

Overcoming Challenges

Running a Catholic magazine in the volatile political climate of the 1920s and 1930s was no easy task. Kolbe faced frequent obstacles, from financial difficulties to censorship attempts by authorities wary of religious influence.

One particularly trying moment came in 1924 when a paper shortage threatened to halt publication. The friary had exhausted its funds, and Kolbe's confreres suggested suspending the magazine until resources could be replenished.

Kolbe, however, refused to give up. "If this is the work of the Immaculate, she will not let it fail," he declared. He spent the night in prayer, entrusting the magazine to Mary's care. The next day, a benefactor arrived unexpectedly, offering a donation that was enough to purchase the needed paper.

Such moments of providence reinforced Kolbe's faith and inspired those around him to persevere.

A Global Impact

By the 1930s, the *Knight of the Immaculate* had become one of the most widely read Catholic publications in Poland and was gaining recognition abroad. Its success was a testament to Kolbe's tireless efforts and his innovative approach to Catholic media.

But for Kolbe, the true measure of success was not in numbers but in the lives transformed by the magazine's message. Each copy, he believed, was a seed planted in the soul of a reader, capable of bearing fruit in ways he might never see.

Conversations and Inspirations

Throughout this time, Kolbe's passion for the written word inspired those who worked alongside him. One evening, as the friars were proofreading an issue of the magazine, Brother Stanisław turned to Kolbe. "Father Maximilian," he asked, "do you ever tire of this work? You seem to pour every ounce of yourself into it."

Kolbe looked up from his desk, his eyes bright with conviction.

"How could I tire of serving the Immaculate?" he replied. "Every word we print, every page we send out into the world, is an opportunity to bring someone closer to Christ. That is a privilege, not a burden."

Building Toward a Legacy

The *Knight of the Immaculate* was more than a publication; it was a reflection of Kolbe's unwavering faith and his ability to harness modern tools for the mission of the Church. Through his magazine, Kolbe not only spread devotion to Mary but also laid the groundwork for a Catholic media network that would continue to inspire long after his time.

As we move to the next chapter, we will explore how Kolbe's vision expanded even further with the founding of Niepokalanów, a "City of the Immaculate" that would become a hub for his missionary work and a testament to his extraordinary faith and ingenuity.

Chapter 5: Expanding the Mission

The Birth of Niepokalanów: "City of the Immaculate"

In the mid-1920s, Maximilian Kolbe's ambitions for the *Militia Immaculatae* had outgrown the friary in Grodno. While the friars worked tirelessly to produce and distribute *Knight of the Immaculate*, demand for the magazine surged, requiring more space, hands, and equipment. Kolbe envisioned not just a publishing house but a spiritual hub—a place where evangelization efforts could flourish.

In 1927, Kolbe's prayers were answered when Prince Jan Drucki-Lubecki donated a plot of land in Teresin, near Warsaw. This barren and wooded area would soon become Niepokalanów, the "City of the Immaculate." From the start, Kolbe made it clear that the new friary would be no ordinary monastery. "This will be a city dedicated entirely to the Immaculate," he told his brothers. "Every building, every effort, will be for her glory."

Building from Scratch

The first friars arrived in Niepokalanów with little more than faith and determination. They slept in makeshift shelters, braving harsh winters and rough conditions. Kolbe, who shared their hardships, inspired them with his unwavering spirit.

"We are building not just with bricks, but with trust in the Immaculate," Kolbe reminded them one evening as they gathered for prayer under the open sky.

By 1930, Niepokalanów had grown into a bustling spiritual and industrial center. It housed a large printing press, dormitories for the friars, workshops, and a chapel at its heart. The friary grew rapidly, attracting vocations from all over Poland. At its peak, it was home to nearly 800 friars, making it one of the largest monasteries in the world.

The daily life in Niepokalanów was a harmonious blend of prayer and work.

Each friar, regardless of rank, took part in the physical labor. Some worked in the printing press, others in the gardens or workshops, and still others in the kitchens. The friars' humility and dedication mirrored Kolbe's own example.

Brother Wojciech, who joined Niepokalanów in 1928, recalled Kolbe's personal touch: "Father Maximilian was always the first to rise and the last to sleep. He worked alongside us, never asking us to do what he himself wouldn't. He taught us to see every task, no matter how mundane, as an act of devotion."

Niepokalanów's Spiritual Vibrancy

Despite its industrial activities, Niepokalanów remained a deeply spiritual place. The friars gathered daily for Mass, the Rosary, and adoration of the Blessed Sacrament. Kolbe insisted that prayer was the cornerstone of their mission.

One day, a young novice approached Kolbe, concerned about balancing work and prayer. "Father, how can we focus on the Immaculate when we are always so busy?"

Kolbe smiled gently and replied, "Every action, no matter how small, becomes prayer when offered to the Immaculate.

When you print a page or sweep the floor, do it with love for her, and you are praying."

This spiritual ethos permeated Niepokalanów, turning it into a beacon of hope for the Catholic Church in Poland and beyond.

A Missionary's Call to Japan

While Niepokalanów flourished, Kolbe's heart burned with a desire to expand the *Militia Immaculatae* globally. He believed that Marian devotion could transform not just Poland but the world. In 1930, this conviction led him to embark on a missionary journey to Japan—a bold decision given the cultural and religious differences he would face.

Kolbe arrived in Nagasaki in April 1930, accompanied by four friars. None of them spoke Japanese, and they had limited resources. The challenges were immense. Japan was a predominantly Buddhist country with a small and often persecuted Catholic minority. Many questioned Kolbe's decision to plant a Marian mission in such unwelcoming soil.

But Kolbe, undeterred, saw an opportunity to spread the Gospel. "The Immaculate has prepared hearts here," he told his companions. "We only need to trust her guidance."

Founding the Garden of the Immaculate

Kolbe began by learning Japanese, immersing himself in the culture and building relationships with local Catholics. He quickly realized that the key to evangelization lay in adapting his methods to the local context. With this in mind, he established a publishing house in Nagasaki to produce a Japanese edition of *Knight of the Immaculate.*

Securing a location for the mission proved challenging. After much prayer, Kolbe chose a plot of land on a mountainside overlooking Nagasaki.

Local advisors warned him that the area was too steep and prone to landslides, but Kolbe remained steadfast.

"This is where the Immaculate wants us to be," he declared.

Years later, Kolbe's choice would prove providential. When the atomic bomb devastated Nagasaki in 1945, the mission on the mountainside remained miraculously intact, shielding its inhabitants from the worst of the blast.

Challenges and Triumphs in Japan

Kolbe's mission faced numerous obstacles. Cultural barriers, financial constraints, and skepticism from local authorities tested his resolve. Yet, his humility and perseverance won the hearts of many.

One story from this period highlights Kolbe's resourcefulness. When the mission's printing press broke down, Kolbe and the friars lacked the funds for repairs. Undeterred, Kolbe wrote to benefactors in Poland, explaining the situation. Within weeks, donations arrived, allowing the press to resume operation.

Through these trials, Kolbe's faith never wavered. "Difficulties," he told his companions, "are simply opportunities for the Immaculate to show her power."

A Growing Influence

Under Kolbe's leadership, the Japanese edition of *Knight of the Immaculate* gained a loyal readership. Written in simple yet profound language, it resonated with both Catholics and non-Catholics. The magazine's articles addressed universal themes—hope, forgiveness, and the search for truth—making it accessible to a diverse audience.

One reader, a young Buddhist woman, wrote to Kolbe, expressing her admiration for the magazine's message of love and peace. Moved by her letter, Kolbe invited her to visit the mission. Their conversations led to her eventual conversion, a testament to Kolbe's gentle yet persuasive approach to evangelization.

Dialogues of Faith

Kolbe's interactions in Japan often showcased his ability to bridge cultural divides. During a conversation with a local scholar, who was intrigued by Catholicism but skeptical of its doctrines, Kolbe patiently explained his beliefs.

"Father Kolbe," the scholar said, "how can you claim that one God is responsible for everything in this vast universe?"

Kolbe paused thoughtfully before replying, "Imagine a single ray of sunlight illuminating an entire garden. Though the garden is vast and filled with countless plants, it is one source that gives it life. So it is with God and creation."

The scholar nodded, visibly impressed by Kolbe's clarity and humility.

Legacy of the Mission in Japan

Kolbe's efforts in Japan laid the foundation for a thriving Catholic community. The mission he established in Nagasaki became a center of Marian devotion and evangelization, reflecting his unwavering faith and ingenuity.

Though his time in Japan was relatively short—he returned to Poland in 1936—Kolbe left an indelible mark. The friars who remained continued his work, inspired by his vision and leadership.

Back to Poland: Expanding the Vision

Upon returning to Niepokalanów, Kolbe found the friary flourishing but also facing new challenges. The political climate in Europe was becoming increasingly volatile, and the Church in Poland faced mounting pressures. Yet, Kolbe remained focused on his mission.

His experiences in Japan had deepened his understanding of global evangelization. He encouraged the friars to think beyond Poland, urging them to see the *Militia Immaculatae* as a worldwide movement.

Setting the Stage for Greater Sacrifices

Kolbe's work in Niepokalanów and Japan showcased his boundless energy and vision. But these accomplishments were only a prelude to the greatest chapter of his life—a chapter defined by sacrifice and love in the face of unimaginable darkness.

As we transition to the next chapter, we will explore how Kolbe's unwavering faith and leadership prepared him for the trials of the Nazi occupation and his ultimate martyrdom in Auschwitz.

Chapter 6: Under Nazi Occupation

The Storm of War Descends

On September 1, 1939, the tranquility of Niepokalanów was shattered as Nazi Germany invaded Poland, marking the beginning of World War II. The once-bustling friary found itself in the midst of a nation under siege. The skies above filled with the roar of Luftwaffe bombers, and the ground trembled under the advance of German tanks. For many Poles, this was the start of a harrowing chapter of occupation and suffering.

Niepokalanów, with its sprawling facilities and community of friars, was not spared. The invasion brought widespread chaos, with families fleeing bombed-out cities and seeking refuge in the countryside. Father Maximilian Kolbe, who had recently returned from Japan, stood at the helm of the friary, rallying his brothers in faith to meet the crisis head-on.

The Nazi Occupation and Its Impact

Under Nazi rule, Poland became a land of oppression. Churches were desecrated, priests were arrested, and Catholic institutions were either shut down or severely restricted. Niepokalanów, however, remained a beacon of hope. Despite the constant threat of Nazi scrutiny, Kolbe refused to let the friary succumb to despair.

The friary soon became a sanctuary for those fleeing persecution. Jews, Catholics, and political refugees all found solace within its walls. At its peak, Niepokalanów sheltered over 3,000 refugees, including 1,500 Jews.

Kolbe's leadership during this time was marked by both courage and ingenuity. He recognized the risks of harboring Jews under the watchful eye of the Gestapo but was unwavering in his resolve. "We are all children of God," he told his brothers one evening. "No matter the cost, we must protect those who come to us seeking refuge."

Sheltering Refugees: Acts of Defiance

Niepokalanów's efforts to aid refugees required careful planning and secrecy. The friars organized food distribution, provided medical care, and even forged documents to help Jews escape detection. Kolbe himself oversaw these operations, ensuring that everyone, regardless of faith or background, was treated with dignity.

One cold November evening, a Jewish mother and her two young children arrived at the friary's gates, their faces etched with fear and exhaustion. A friar rushed to inform Kolbe, who immediately came to greet them.

"Welcome," he said softly, kneeling to the children's level. "You are safe here."

The mother, overcome with emotion, whispered, "But Father, if they find us here, they will kill you too."

Kolbe placed a reassuring hand on her shoulder. "My dear sister, do not be afraid. The Immaculate watches over us. We are in God's hands."

This scene repeated itself countless times as Kolbe and his brothers offered sanctuary to the most vulnerable.

Resistance Through Faith

Kolbe's resistance to the Nazis extended beyond sheltering refugees. He believed that the greatest weapon against evil was unwavering faith. Despite the oppressive environment, he continued to print *Knight of the Immaculate,* using its pages to inspire hope and courage among Poles.

In one edition, Kolbe wrote:
"Darkness has fallen over our land, but remember, no darkness can extinguish the light of Christ. Stand firm in your faith, for it

is the anchor that will see us through this storm."

The magazine's distribution became a clandestine operation, with copies smuggled into occupied cities and even concentration camps. These acts of defiance did not go unnoticed by the Nazis, who increasingly viewed Niepokalanów as a threat.

Facing Nazi Persecution

The Gestapo raided Niepokalanów multiple times, searching for evidence of anti-Nazi activities. During one such raid in February 1941, Kolbe was arrested along with several friars. The soldiers stormed into his office, overturning furniture and confiscating documents.

A Gestapo officer sneered at Kolbe, "So, you think you can defy the Reich with your little magazine?"

Kolbe, calm and composed, replied, "The truth cannot be silenced, not by force, nor fear."

This defiance earned him a brutal beating, but Kolbe remained steadfast. After several weeks in prison, he was released, only to return to Niepokalanów and resume his work.

Sacrifices for the Greater Good

Kolbe's commitment to protecting others often came at a personal cost. Food and resources were scarce, yet he insisted that the friary's supplies be shared with refugees.

One winter, when rations ran dangerously low, a friar approached Kolbe with concern. "Father, if we continue like this, we won't have enough to feed ourselves."

Kolbe looked at him with a serene smile. "The Immaculate will provide. Let us not worry about tomorrow but focus on what we can do today."

True to his words, donations arrived unexpectedly from local farmers and sympathetic neighbors, allowing the friary to continue its mission.

Witnessing to Faith Amid Darkness

Kolbe's unwavering faith became a source of inspiration for those around him. Many refugees, including Jews who had little reason to trust Christians after years of persecution, were moved by his compassion.

Rabbi Jacob Silverman, who sought refuge in Niepokalanów, later recalled: "Father Kolbe was a man of extraordinary kindness.

He did not see Jews or Catholics, only human beings. In a time of hatred, he stood as a beacon of love."

Preparing for the Ultimate Sacrifice

As the war intensified, so did the Nazis' crackdown on Catholic institutions. By late 1941, it became clear that Niepokalanów's days as a sanctuary were numbered. Kolbe, however, remained undeterred.

During a meeting with his brothers, he spoke of the need for courage in the face of adversity. "We may face great trials ahead," he said. "But remember, our mission is to serve, no matter the cost. Let us entrust everything to the Immaculate."

His words proved prophetic. On February 17, 1941, the Gestapo returned to Niepokalanów, arresting Kolbe and several friars. This time, there would be no release.

Legacy of Courage

Kolbe's actions during the Nazi occupation left an indelible mark on those who knew him. His courage, compassion, and unshakable faith stood in stark contrast to the hatred and violence of the time.

As we move into the next chapter, we will follow Kolbe's journey to Auschwitz, where his ultimate sacrifice would define his legacy as a martyr of charity.

Chapter 7: A Witness to Hope in Auschwitz

Arrest and Imprisonment

On February 17, 1941, the Gestapo stormed Niepokalanów for the final time. Father Maximilian Kolbe and several friars were arrested. While others were taken to various prisons, Kolbe's path led him to the dreaded Auschwitz concentration camp, a place synonymous with death and despair.

As Kolbe was herded into a cramped train car with other prisoners, the air thick with fear and stench, his presence exuded a strange calm. A young prisoner whispered to him, "Father, do you think we will survive this journey?"

Kolbe replied gently, "We do not walk alone. Trust in the Immaculate; she watches over us, even in this darkness."

When the train finally stopped at Auschwitz, the men were ordered out with screams and gunfire. Stripped of their belongings, dignity, and even their names, the prisoners were reduced to mere numbers. Kolbe became *Prisoner 16670*.

Arrival at Auschwitz

Auschwitz was a world of inhumanity. Upon arrival, Kolbe and the other prisoners were subjected to brutal beatings and hours of forced labor. The guards took particular pleasure in breaking the spirits of new arrivals.

Kolbe's calm demeanor, however, unsettled them. When a guard struck him across the face for not responding quickly enough, Kolbe looked up and said, "May God forgive you." The guard, startled by this response, paused before striking him again.

Despite the horrors surrounding him, Kolbe's faith remained unshaken.

He was assigned to manual labor, including carrying heavy logs, a task that left many men broken. Witnesses later recounted how Kolbe encouraged others to keep going, offering whispered prayers and words of hope.

A Light in the Darkness

Kolbe's spiritual leadership in Auschwitz became a beacon of hope for many. In the overcrowded barracks, where despair often claimed lives faster than disease, Kolbe quietly ministered to his fellow prisoners.

Each night, after the guards' rounds, Kolbe would gather small groups of men to pray. His voice, soft but steady, carried messages of hope. "This suffering," he would say, "is not the end. It is a path to a greater glory, a union with Christ who suffered for us all."

One prisoner, Andrzej, later recalled: "In the midst of hell, Father Kolbe reminded us that we were still human. He gave us the strength to endure another day."

Kolbe's acts of compassion extended beyond prayer. Despite the meager rations, he often gave his bread to those weaker than himself. When prisoners fell ill, Kolbe tended to them, risking punishment to provide what little comfort he could.

The Ultimate Test of Love

By July 1941, the oppressive heat and inhuman conditions had reached a breaking point in Auschwitz. After an inmate from Kolbe's barracks escaped, the camp's deputy commandant, Karl Fritzsch, ordered a reprisal. Ten men were to be chosen at random to die in the starvation bunker, a fate designed to instill terror and prevent further escapes.

The prisoners were assembled in the yard, and Fritzsch walked among them, pointing at men to fill his quota. The chosen men fell to their knees, weeping and begging for their lives.

Among them was Franciszek Gajowniczek, a Polish army sergeant.

Gajowniczek cried out, "My wife! My children! What will they do without me?" His anguish echoed through the yard.

It was then that Kolbe stepped forward. The guards froze, stunned by his audacity. Prisoners held their breath, knowing that any act of defiance could result in immediate execution.

Kolbe spoke calmly but firmly. "I am a Catholic priest. Let me take his place. He has a family; I do not."

Fritzsch stared at Kolbe, his expression a mix of confusion and contempt. "Who are you to make such a request?" he sneered.

Kolbe replied, "I am a priest. It is my duty to serve others, even to the point of death."

After a tense pause, Fritzsch agreed, waving Gajowniczek back into the line. Kolbe, now one of the condemned, walked with the other nine men to the starvation bunker, his face serene as if he were heading to prayer.

The Starvation Bunker

The starvation bunker was a small, dark cell where prisoners were left without food or water until they succumbed to death. For most, it was a place of despair, filled with cries of agony. But with Kolbe among them, the bunker became something entirely different.

Kolbe led the men in prayer and hymns. Instead of screams, the guards reported hearing chants of praise coming from the cell. One guard, clearly disturbed, remarked to another, "This priest… he's turning the bunker into a church."

The transformation of the starvation bunker became the talk of Auschwitz.

Prisoners whispered of Kolbe's faith and courage, drawing strength from his example.

Final Days

After two weeks, only Kolbe and a few others were still alive. The guards, impatient to clear the bunker for the next group of victims, decided to hasten their deaths with lethal injections of carbolic acid.

On August 14, 1941, a guard entered the bunker with a syringe. Kolbe, emaciated but composed, raised his arm without resistance. Witnesses later said that his face radiated peace as he whispered, "Ave Maria."

Kolbe's death was not the end of his influence. His courage and sacrifice left an indelible mark on everyone who witnessed it.

The Life Saved

Franciszek Gajowniczek, the man for whom Kolbe gave his life, survived Auschwitz and lived to tell Kolbe's story to the world. He would later say, "I owe him my life. He saved me, and in doing so, he showed the world what it means to love selflessly."

Gajowniczek spent the rest of his life honoring Kolbe's memory, speaking at events and sharing his testimony. His survival became a living testament to Kolbe's ultimate act of charity.

A Legacy of Hope

Kolbe's actions in Auschwitz exemplified the triumph of love over hate, faith over fear. In a place designed to strip humanity from its prisoners, he reminded others of their inherent dignity. His life and death continue to inspire millions, a shining example of what it means to live for others.

Chapter 8: Echoes of Heroism: Survivors' Testimonies

A Light in the Darkness

The death of Father Maximilian Kolbe reverberated through the walls of Auschwitz like a solemn hymn of hope. Though his body had succumbed to the cruelty of the Nazis, his spirit remained palpable, etched into the memories of those who had witnessed his final days.

Among these witnesses was Franciszek Gajowniczek, the man whose life Kolbe had saved. Sitting in a modest home years after the war, Gajowniczek struggled to recount the moment that had forever altered his life. "How do you describe someone who willingly gave his life for yours?" he asked, his voice trembling. "There are no words."

Kolbe's sacrifice had not only spared Gajowniczek's life but also ignited a spark of hope in a place designed to extinguish it. Through the testimonies of survivors, the echoes of Kolbe's heroism continued to resonate far beyond the barbed wire of Auschwitz.

Franciszek Gajowniczek's Testimony

Franciszek Gajowniczek was a Polish army sergeant, arrested by the Gestapo and imprisoned in Auschwitz for aiding the resistance. In July 1941, after a prisoner escaped, the camp commandant selected ten men to die by starvation as a grim warning to others.

"I was just one among many," Gajowniczek recalled. "When they called my name, I froze. I thought of my wife, my children. I begged, 'My family! My poor family!'"

As the guards dragged him forward, a figure stepped out of line.

It was Kolbe. His voice was calm but resolute. "I am a Catholic priest," he said. "I want to take this man's place. He has a wife and children. I have no one."

Gajowniczek watched in stunned silence as Kolbe spoke to the commandant. "It was as if he didn't fear death," he said. "He stood there, tall and composed, like a man on a mission."

To everyone's astonishment, the commandant agreed. Gajowniczek was sent back to the barracks, and Kolbe took his place in the starvation bunker.

For the rest of his life, Gajowniczek carried the weight of Kolbe's sacrifice. "Every breath I take is because of him," he said. "I've tried to live a life worthy of that gift."

Other Survivors Speak

Kolbe's influence extended far beyond Gajowniczek. Survivors who shared the same barracks or witnessed his actions described him as a beacon of light in the darkest of times.

One survivor, a young man named Jerzy, recalled Kolbe's presence during roll calls. "He was always there, helping the weak stand, whispering prayers to those who couldn't go on," Jerzy said. "He made us feel like human beings, even when the world wanted us to forget we were."

Another prisoner, an elderly woman who worked in the camp kitchen, spoke of Kolbe's remarkable demeanor. "I saw him once when he came to collect the meager rations for his block," she said. "His face was serene, almost radiant. He greeted the guards with kindness, even though they treated him like dirt."

Jerzy described the day he saw Kolbe in the starvation bunker. "I was in the block next to it," he said. "We could hear them singing hymns. It was unbelievable—like a miracle. How could they sing when they were starving to death?"

Kolbe's Legacy of Resilience

The survivors' stories highlight Kolbe's extraordinary ability to inspire resilience. His unwavering faith and selflessness transformed a place of despair into a sanctuary of hope, even if only for a moment.

Years later, Gajowniczek became one of Kolbe's most vocal proponents. "He didn't just save me," Gajowniczek said. "He saved my faith, my hope. In that moment, he reminded me that love can conquer even the greatest evil."

Gajowniczek spent decades sharing Kolbe's story, visiting schools, churches, and conferences. His life became a living testimony to Kolbe's sacrifice.

Kolbe's Impact Beyond Auschwitz

The echoes of Kolbe's heroism extended beyond the lives of survivors. His story became a symbol of love's triumph over hate, inspiring millions around the world.

In a post-war interview, a camp guard who had witnessed Kolbe's actions admitted, "I didn't understand him then. But now, I see he was a saint. He had something we couldn't take away—his faith."

Kolbe's example has inspired countless acts of courage and compassion. From humanitarian workers to religious leaders, many have drawn strength from his legacy.

One notable instance occurred in the 1980s, when a group of Polish Solidarity members, facing imprisonment for their resistance to the Communist regime, invoked Kolbe's name. "He showed us that one man's courage can inspire a movement," one member said.

A Message for All Generations

Kolbe's story is not just one of sacrifice; it is a call to action. His life challenges us to confront hatred with love, despair with hope, and cruelty with compassion.

In a world still grappling with division and suffering, Kolbe's example shines as a timeless reminder of what it means to live for others. His sacrifice, though rooted in a specific moment in history, transcends time, offering hope and inspiration to generations yet to come.

Auschwitz as Sacred Ground

Today, Auschwitz stands as a solemn reminder of humanity's capacity for evil—and for good. Visitors often stop at Block 11, the site of the starvation bunker, to pay their respects to Kolbe.

Franciszek Gajowniczek, until his death in 1995, made an annual pilgrimage to Auschwitz. "This place, which once symbolized death, now reminds me of life," he said. "It reminds me of the love that Father Kolbe showed, a love that can never be extinguished."

As Gajowniczek knelt before the bunker, tears streaming down his face, he whispered, "Thank you, Father Kolbe. You taught me what it means to live."

A Legacy That Lives On

Kolbe's actions at Auschwitz were not just heroic—they were transformative. His courage and faith in the face of unimaginable suffering remind us that even in the darkest moments, the light of love can shine through.

The testimonies of those who knew him, and those who were saved by him, ensure that his legacy will never be forgotten. Father Maximilian Kolbe may have died in Auschwitz, but his spirit lives on, a witness to the power of selfless love.

Chapter 9: The Path to Sainthood

A Death That Reverberated Beyond Auschwitz

Father Maximilian Kolbe's death in Auschwitz was not the end of his story—it was the beginning of a spiritual legacy that transcended time and place. His final act of selfless love set in motion a ripple effect that would eventually lead the Catholic Church to honor him as one of its greatest saints.

In the immediate aftermath of the war, survivors of Auschwitz began sharing Kolbe's story, recounting his courage, compassion, and unwavering faith. Testimonies poured in from those who had witnessed his sacrifice, particularly Franciszek Gajowniczek, whose life Kolbe had saved. "He died so that I could live," Gajowniczek often said. "His love knew no bounds."

The world slowly began to recognize that Kolbe's act of heroism was not just an isolated moment but a reflection of a life dedicated to the service of others.

The Initial Steps Toward Recognition

The process of recognizing Kolbe's sanctity began in earnest in 1948, just three years after the end of World War II. The Franciscan Order, deeply moved by Kolbe's martyrdom, petitioned the Vatican to open a cause for his beatification.

In 1955, Pope Pius XII officially granted the title of "Servant of God" to Kolbe, the first step in the rigorous process of sainthood. This title acknowledged Kolbe's virtuous life and his willingness to die for another.

By this time, accounts of Kolbe's actions in Auschwitz had reached the broader Catholic community. Franciszek Gajowniczek became one of the most vocal proponents of Kolbe's cause, traveling across Poland and Europe to share the story of the priest who had saved his life. "He wasn't just a man," Gajowniczek said during a speech at a Catholic conference. "He was a reflection of Christ's love in the world."

Testimonies of Miracles

One of the key requirements for sainthood is the verification of miracles attributed to the intercession of the candidate. As news of Kolbe's story spread, countless people began praying for his intercession, and numerous miracles were reported.

Among the most notable was the case of a young woman in Poland who had been diagnosed with an aggressive form of cancer. Her family prayed fervently to Kolbe, asking for his intercession. Against all medical odds, her cancer disappeared, leaving doctors baffled. This event was meticulously investigated by the Church and eventually recognized as a miracle.

Another story came from Japan, where Kolbe had once served as a missionary. A small Catholic community in Nagasaki reported that their prayers to Kolbe had protected them from a devastating typhoon. "Father Kolbe's spirit is with us," one elderly parishioner said.

Beatification by Pope Paul VI

On October 17, 1971, Pope Paul VI officially beatified Maximilian Kolbe, declaring him "Blessed." The ceremony, held in St. Peter's Basilica, was attended by thousands, including Gajowniczek, who stood weeping in the crowd.

During his homily, Pope Paul VI described Kolbe as "a shining example of Christian love," emphasizing that his sacrifice was not only heroic but also deeply rooted in his faith. "He gave his life freely, not out of compulsion but out of love for his fellow man and his God," the Pope said.

The beatification was a significant milestone, but the journey to full sainthood was not yet complete.

Pope John Paul II and the Canonization Process

The final steps toward Kolbe's canonization were taken under the papacy of Pope John Paul II, himself a Polish priest deeply inspired by Kolbe's life. John Paul II had grown up hearing about Kolbe's work in Niepokalanów and his sacrifice in Auschwitz. For the Pope, Kolbe's story was deeply personal.

During a visit to Auschwitz in 1979, John Paul II paused at the site of the starvation bunker where Kolbe had died. Kneeling in prayer, he later described the moment as "standing on holy ground." He declared Kolbe's actions "a victory of love over hate, a testimony to the power of faith."

In 1980, the Vatican formally recognized a second miracle attributed to Kolbe's intercession, clearing the way for his canonization. This miracle involved a young woman in Brazil who had been in a coma following a severe accident. Her recovery, which doctors could not explain, was attributed to prayers made to Kolbe.

Declared a Martyr of Charity

On October 10, 1982, Pope John Paul II canonized Maximilian Kolbe in a ceremony attended by tens of thousands, including many Auschwitz survivors. The event was a moment of profound significance, not only for the Catholic Church but also for the world.

In his homily, Pope John Paul II bestowed upon Kolbe the title "Martyr of Charity," a designation that reflected the unique nature of his sacrifice. "He did not die because he was hated," the Pope said. "He died because he loved."

Gajowniczek, then 81 years old, was present at the canonization. As he listened to the Pope's words, tears streamed down his face. "I owe my life to him," he told reporters afterward. "Now the whole world knows what he did."

Kolbe's Influence on the Modern World

The canonization of Maximilian Kolbe cemented his place as a universal symbol of love and selflessness. His story has since inspired countless individuals, from laypeople to world leaders.

In Poland, Niepokalanów became a major pilgrimage site, drawing visitors from around the globe. The Franciscan friary, once a humble center of Marian devotion, now stands as a testament to Kolbe's enduring legacy.

Kolbe's influence extended to social justice movements, with many drawing parallels between his actions and the fight against oppression and injustice. His life became a touchstone for those working to promote peace and reconciliation in a divided world.

The Legacy of a Saint

Father Maximilian Kolbe's journey from Auschwitz to sainthood is a story of unwavering faith, boundless love, and extraordinary courage. His canonization was not merely an acknowledgment of his martyrdom but a celebration of a life dedicated to serving others.

In his closing remarks at the canonization ceremony, Pope John Paul II addressed the global audience: "Let us remember that Maximilian Kolbe's sacrifice was not an end but a beginning. His life calls us to be instruments of love, to resist hatred, and to build a world rooted in compassion."

Today, Kolbe's story continues to inspire, reminding us that even in the darkest of times, the light of love can prevail.

Dialogue and Reflection

During a post-canonization interview, a journalist asked Franciszek Gajowniczek, "What would you say to Father Kolbe if you could speak to him now?"

Gajowniczek paused, his voice breaking. "I would say thank you," he said. "Not just for saving my life, but for teaching me what it means to live with purpose. He showed us all that love is stronger than hate."

Chapter 10: Global Influence

A Saint for the Modern World

The life and sacrifice of Saint Maximilian Kolbe resonate far beyond the confines of his time and place. Canonized as a "Martyr of Charity," his influence extends globally, touching lives across diverse cultures, movements, and struggles. From pro-life advocacy to addiction recovery and modern Marian devotion, Kolbe's legacy remains a guiding light in the challenges of the modern era.

In an era marked by division and moral complexities, Kolbe's story has been embraced by millions as a symbol of hope, love, and faith. His teachings and example have inspired initiatives and movements that continue to shape lives and bring people closer to the ideals he so passionately lived and died for.

Patron Saint of Our Times

Upon his canonization, the Catholic Church declared Maximilian Kolbe the patron saint of drug addicts, prisoners, families, and the pro-life movement. Each of these designations reflects an aspect of Kolbe's life and mission.

As the patron of drug addicts, Kolbe's intercession has been sought by countless individuals battling addiction. His unwavering dedication to self-discipline and his Marian devotion resonate deeply with those seeking to overcome personal struggles. In rehabilitation centers worldwide, his story is shared as a source of strength.

In a small recovery center in California, a counselor recalls an impactful moment: "I shared Kolbe's story with a group of recovering addicts. They were moved by his selflessness and faith. One man said, 'If someone like him could overcome suffering and still give so much, then I can find strength too.'"

As the patron of prisoners, Kolbe's experiences in Auschwitz have provided hope and redemption for those incarcerated. His choice to sacrifice himself for another stands as a testament to the value of every human life, regardless of circumstances. Many prison ministries have adopted Kolbe's teachings, reminding inmates that transformation and spiritual freedom are always possible.

Pro-Life Advocacy: A Testament to the Sanctity of Life

Kolbe's profound respect for the sanctity of life has made him an icon in the pro-life movement. His willingness to lay down his life for another person serves as a reminder of the inherent value of every human being. Pro-life advocates frequently invoke his name in their efforts to protect the unborn, the elderly, and the vulnerable.

At a pro-life rally in Poland, a young woman shared how Kolbe's story inspired her activism: "I was hesitant to get involved in this cause, but when I read about Kolbe's sacrifice, I realized that defending life, no matter how difficult, is a call to love. His courage gave me courage."

Kolbe's teachings on love and sacrifice have also influenced organizations that work with expectant mothers, encouraging them to choose life even in the face of adversity. The phrase "Kolbe's courage" has become a rallying cry for many pro-life advocates.

Addiction Recovery: A Journey of Hope

Kolbe's life also provides solace and strength for those battling addiction. His deep devotion to the Immaculate Virgin and his emphasis on self-discipline offer a spiritual framework for individuals seeking recovery.

Many addiction recovery programs have adopted Kolbe's teachings, emphasizing the importance of surrendering to divine grace and finding strength through faith. His intercession has been credited with miraculous recoveries, leading to his growing popularity among those struggling with substance abuse.

In Brazil, a man recovering from a decade-long battle with alcoholism shared his story: "I prayed to Saint Maximilian Kolbe every day, asking for his guidance. Slowly, I found the strength to overcome my addiction. I feel like he was walking with me every step of the way."

Kolbe's influence has extended to recovery centers, where his story is shared as a source of inspiration. A counselor in Ireland reflected, "Kolbe teaches us that no matter how broken we feel, redemption is always possible. His life is a testament to the power of grace."

Modern Marian Devotion: The Army of the Immaculate

Kolbe's unwavering devotion to the Virgin Mary continues to inspire Marian movements worldwide. The Militia Immaculatae, which he founded, has grown into an international organization with millions of members dedicated to spreading Marian devotion and living according to her example.

In a Marian congress held in Nagasaki, Japan, a young participant shared how Kolbe's devotion to Mary had transformed her faith: "Through Saint Maximilian Kolbe, I learned to see Mary not just as a figure in the Bible but as a mother who walks with me every day."

Kolbe's teachings on the Immaculate Conception remain a cornerstone of Marian theology. His writings emphasize Mary's role as a mediator of grace, inspiring theologians and laypeople alike to deepen their devotion.

The global reach of the Militia Immaculatae is a testament to Kolbe's vision. From small prayer groups in rural villages to large gatherings in urban centers, the movement continues to promote faith, love, and service through Mary's intercession.

Inspiring Resilience in Modern Challenges

Kolbe's life has become a beacon of hope in times of crisis. His teachings on love, sacrifice, and perseverance resonate deeply with individuals and communities facing hardship.

In conflict zones, his story has been shared as a symbol of resistance against hate and oppression. Humanitarian organizations have drawn inspiration from Kolbe's example, emphasizing the importance of compassion and selflessness in their work.

A social worker in Syria reflected, "Kolbe's story reminds us that even in the darkest moments, love can triumph. His example gives us the courage to keep going, even when the odds seem insurmountable."

Dialogues that Echo Through Generations

One of the most touching accounts comes from a conversation between a priest and a recovering addict who had found hope through Kolbe's story.

"Father, do you think someone like me could ever be worthy of redemption?" the man asked, tears streaming down his face.

The priest smiled gently. "Saint Maximilian Kolbe once said that love alone creates. If you open your heart to God's love, you'll find that redemption is not just possible—it's inevitable."

A Saint for All

Saint Maximilian Kolbe's global influence lies in his ability to transcend boundaries. His life speaks to the universal human experience, reminding us of the power of love, faith, and courage.

From pro-life advocates to addiction recovery programs, from Marian devotees to prisoners seeking hope, Kolbe's story continues to inspire and transform lives.

His legacy is a testament to the enduring power of grace and the unyielding strength of the human spirit.

As one admirer aptly said, "Saint Maximilian Kolbe's life was a masterpiece of love. In a world that often forgets how to love, his story reminds us of what it truly means to be human."

Chapter 11: The Mystical Depths of Kolbe's Teachings

Saint Maximilian Kolbe's spiritual legacy is built not only on his heroic sacrifice but also on his profound theological insights, which remain a source of inspiration for theologians and laypeople alike. His teachings on suffering, love, and Marian devotion reflect the depth of his relationship with God and the Virgin Mary, offering a rich tapestry of wisdom for those seeking to deepen their faith.

Kolbe's theology was neither abstract nor inaccessible. It emerged from his lived experiences, his writings, and his unwavering devotion. His reflections on suffering and the redemptive power of love provide a roadmap for navigating life's challenges, while his unique Marian theology underscores the central role of the Immaculate Conception in salvation history.

The Theology of Suffering and Redemptive Love

For Kolbe, suffering was not a meaningless burden but a profound opportunity to participate in Christ's redemptive mission. This belief was rooted in his deep understanding of the mystery of the Cross. He often emphasized that suffering, when united with love, becomes a powerful force for transformation and redemption.

In one of his writings, Kolbe remarked, "Love alone creates. Even in suffering, it is love that gives it purpose and meaning. To suffer for others, to love others through one's pain, is to touch the heart of Christ's sacrifice."

This perspective was not mere theory for Kolbe; it was a reality he lived daily, especially during his time in Auschwitz. In the starvation bunker, he transformed a place of despair into a sanctuary of hope by leading his fellow prisoners in prayers and hymns. His ability to radiate love amidst unimaginable suffering illustrated the transformative power of his theology.

One survivor later recalled, "In that bunker, where death seemed inevitable, Father Kolbe's presence was a reminder that love can conquer even the darkest moments. His prayers lifted our spirits, and his unwavering faith gave us strength."

Kolbe's reflections on suffering also resonate with those facing personal trials.

His belief that suffering can be offered as a gift to God has inspired countless individuals to find hope and purpose in their struggles.

A Love That Redeems

Central to Kolbe's theology was the idea that love is not only redemptive but also transformative. For him, love was the ultimate expression of faith, a force capable of breaking down barriers and bringing people closer to God.

Kolbe often described love as a fire that consumes selfishness and purifies the soul. He wrote, "The love that Christ showed on the Cross is the same love we are called to imitate. It is a love that gives without counting the cost, that sacrifices without seeking reward."

This understanding of love was evident in his everyday actions, from his care for his fellow friars at Niepokalanów to his selfless decision to take the place of Franciszek Gajowniczek in Auschwitz. Kolbe's love was not limited to grand gestures; it was also expressed in small, everyday acts of kindness that reflected his commitment to living the Gospel.

Kolbe's Unique Devotion to the Immaculate Conception

Kolbe's theology was deeply Marian, centered on his unwavering devotion to the Immaculate Conception. For him, the Virgin Mary was not only the mother of Christ but also the mediator of all graces, a bridge between humanity and God.

Kolbe's understanding of Mary's role in salvation history was profoundly influenced by his own mystical experiences. One of the most pivotal moments in his life was the vision he received as a child, in which the Virgin Mary offered him two crowns—one white, symbolizing purity, and one red, symbolizing martyrdom.

This vision shaped his vocation and his lifelong devotion to Mary.

In his writings, Kolbe often referred to Mary as the "Immaculata" and emphasized her unique role in God's plan of salvation. He believed that Mary's Immaculate Conception was a testament to God's infinite love and mercy. By preserving her from sin, God provided humanity with a perfect model of faith and obedience.

Kolbe also saw Mary as a powerful intercessor, capable of bringing grace to even the most hardened hearts. He once wrote, "Through the Immaculata, all graces flow. She is the mediatrix of mercy, the mother who leads us to her Son."

This devotion to Mary was not passive; it was active and missionary. Kolbe's founding of the Militia Immaculatae was a reflection of his desire to bring others closer to Christ through Mary. He believed that by consecrating oneself to the Immaculata, one could become a more effective instrument of God's love.

The Immaculate Conception and Catholic Theology

Kolbe's Marian theology has had a lasting impact on Catholic thought, particularly in its emphasis on the Immaculate Conception. His writings have been studied by theologians seeking to understand the depth of Mary's role in salvation history.

One of Kolbe's most profound insights was his belief that Mary's Immaculate Conception was a reflection of God's ultimate plan for humanity. He saw her as the new Eve, whose obedience and purity reversed the disobedience of the first Eve. This understanding aligns with the Church's teachings on Mary but adds a unique perspective that emphasizes her role as a co-redeemer with Christ.

Kolbe also emphasized the importance of consecration to Mary as a means of deepening one's relationship with Christ. He believed that by entrusting oneself to Mary, one could more fully embrace God's will and grow in holiness.

Dialogues that Illuminate His Teachings

Kolbe's profound theology often found expression in his conversations with others. In one instance, a young friar approached him, struggling to understand the meaning of suffering.

"Father Maximilian," the friar asked, "why does God allow us to suffer so much? It feels unbearable at times."

Kolbe smiled gently. "My son, suffering is a mystery, but it is not without purpose.

When we unite our suffering with Christ's, it becomes a gift—a way to love others and draw closer to God. Remember, love alone creates. Even in pain, love can transform and redeem."

Such conversations were not uncommon for Kolbe, who often took the time to guide and inspire those around him. His ability to convey complex theological ideas in simple, relatable terms made his teachings accessible to people from all walks of life.

A Legacy of Mystical Depth

Kolbe's theological insights continue to inspire and challenge believers. His reflections on suffering and love provide a framework for understanding life's challenges, while his Marian devotion offers a pathway to deepening one's faith.

In the years since his death, Kolbe's writings have been studied and celebrated by theologians, clergy, and laypeople alike. His teachings remain a source of inspiration for those seeking to live out their faith with greater devotion and purpose.

As one theologian aptly observed, "Saint Maximilian Kolbe's theology is a bridge between the human and the divine. Through his reflections on suffering, love, and Mary, he offers us a glimpse of the infinite mercy and grace of God."

Chapter 12: Kolbe and the Science of Faith

Saint Maximilian Kolbe's life was an extraordinary interplay of deep faith and sharp intellect. His ability to merge Catholic philosophy with scientific knowledge not only set him apart as a theologian but also as a thinker ahead of his time. Kolbe's contributions to Catholic philosophy and his embrace of scientific inquiry demonstrated a profound commitment to bridging faith and reason, paving the way for a model of intellectual spirituality that remains relevant in the modern world.

The Scholar with a Scientific Mind

Long before his canonization, Kolbe's scholarly pursuits marked him as an exceptional individual. During his studies in Rome, he demonstrated an insatiable curiosity for understanding the world beyond theological dogma. While his primary focus was theology and philosophy, Kolbe was particularly drawn to the natural sciences, especially mathematics, physics, and astronomy.

At the Pontifical Gregorian University and later at the Pontifical University of Saint Bonaventure, Kolbe excelled in his academic endeavors, earning not one but two doctorates—one in theology and the other in philosophy. Yet, his intellectual pursuits were never disconnected from his spiritual life. Kolbe believed that understanding the natural world was another way of glorifying God.

In one of his essays, Kolbe wrote, "The universe is a reflection of the Creator's infinite wisdom and love. To study its laws is to uncover the fingerprints of God Himself." This sentiment revealed his approach to science—not as a threat to faith, but as a complementary path to understanding the divine.

Integrating Science into Faith

Kolbe's scientific perspective was deeply integrated into his ministry. At Niepokalanów, the "City of the Immaculate," he established a printing press and later a radio station—technological advancements that underscored his belief in using modern tools to spread the Gospel. He was fascinated by the potential of these innovations, not only for evangelization but also as a means of connecting people and ideas.

Kolbe's efforts to harness technology for faith extended to his missionary work in Japan. When establishing the Marian center

in Nagasaki, he chose the location based on
his understanding of geographical and
environmental factors, selecting a site
shielded from natural disasters. This
decision was vindicated when the center
survived the atomic bombing of Nagasaki in
1945, an event Kolbe did not live to witness.

Kolbe also envisioned the use of scientific
advancements in broader theological
applications. He saw science as a way to
address modern skepticism and indifference
toward faith. To Kolbe, faith and reason
were not opposing forces but
complementary pathways leading to the
same truth.

A Model for Bridging Faith and Reason

Kolbe's life and work exemplified the harmony between faith and reason. He was a devout Marian theologian, yet he never shied away from engaging with the intellectual challenges of his time. His writings often reflected this balance, offering profound theological insights while remaining grounded in rational discourse.

For example, in one of his articles for *Knight of the Immaculate,* Kolbe addressed the relationship between science and faith, stating:
"Science seeks to understand the how of creation, while faith seeks to understand the

why. Together, they reveal the full grandeur of God's plan for the universe."

This ability to articulate the coexistence of faith and reason made Kolbe a powerful apologist for Catholicism. His approach was particularly effective in countering the atheistic ideologies of his time, which often dismissed religion as incompatible with modern science.

Dialogues and Intellectual Encounters

Kolbe's intellectual pursuits often brought him into dialogue with individuals who questioned or doubted the compatibility of science and faith. One notable instance occurred during his missionary work in Japan, where he encountered a young university professor who identified as an atheist.

The professor, curious but skeptical, asked, "Father Kolbe, how can you, a man of faith, believe in miracles and divine mysteries when science explains so much of the world?"

Kolbe responded with characteristic warmth and wisdom:

"My friend, science indeed explains the laws of the universe, but it does not explain why those laws exist in the first place. Faith answers the deeper questions—questions of purpose, meaning, and love. Together, science and faith paint a fuller picture of reality."

This conversation left a lasting impression on the professor, who later described Kolbe as "a man whose faith was as vast as his intellect."

Kolbe's Philosophical Contributions

Kolbe's contributions to Catholic philosophy were deeply rooted in his understanding of human dignity and divine love. His Marian theology, which emphasized Mary's role as the mediator of all graces, was not merely devotional but also deeply philosophical. He viewed Mary as the bridge between humanity and God, a role that reflected the unity of creation and redemption.

In his philosophical writings, Kolbe often explored the concept of freedom, particularly as it related to the human capacity for self-giving love. He argued that true freedom is not the absence of constraints but the ability to align one's will with God's will. This idea was a cornerstone of his spirituality and influenced his actions, including his ultimate sacrifice in Auschwitz.

Kolbe's integration of philosophy and theology also extended to his reflections on suffering. He viewed suffering as a mystery that could only be understood in the light of Christ's redemptive love. This perspective provided a framework for addressing existential questions, offering hope and meaning in the face of adversity.

Faith and Science in Modern Contexts

Kolbe's insights into the relationship between faith and science have become increasingly relevant in today's world. As scientific advancements continue to reshape society, his belief in the compatibility of these two realms serves as a reminder that faith need not be sidelined in the pursuit of knowledge.

Kolbe's legacy challenges the notion that religion and science are inherently at odds. His life demonstrates that faith can inspire scientific curiosity, and scientific discoveries can deepen one's appreciation for the divine. This holistic approach to understanding the world remains a valuable model for addressing contemporary debates about the role of religion in an increasingly secular society.

A Vision for Intellectual Spirituality

Kolbe's ability to bridge faith and reason offers a blueprint for intellectual spirituality that resonates with modern audiences. His life shows that one can be both deeply devout and intellectually rigorous, embracing the complexities of faith without abandoning critical inquiry.

As one theologian observed, "Saint Maximilian Kolbe exemplifies what it means to be a thinker for God. His integration of science and faith is a testament to the harmony between human reason and divine revelation."

Kolbe's vision continues to inspire scholars, scientists, and believers alike. His contributions to Catholic philosophy and his embrace of scientific knowledge remind us that faith and reason are not competitors but collaborators in the quest for truth.

In celebrating Kolbe's legacy, we are reminded of the profound unity between the spiritual and the intellectual —a unity that reflects the infinite wisdom and love of the Creator. Through his life and teachings,

Kolbe invites us to explore this unity, bridging the gap between faith and reason in our own journeys of discovery.

Conclusion: Living the Kolbe Legacy – Defying Hate with Love in Today's World

Saint Maximilian Kolbe's life, teachings, and ultimate sacrifice are a timeless testament to the power of love, faith, and selflessness in the face of overwhelming adversity. His story is not merely one of personal triumph; it is a profound blueprint for living a life of purpose, courage, and spiritual strength. As we conclude this journey through his remarkable life, the lessons Kolbe offers resonate deeply in a world still grappling with hatred, division, and despair.

Living the Kolbe Legacy: Lessons from His Life

Maximilian Kolbe's story is a luminous example of the transformative power of love. At every stage of his life, Kolbe demonstrated an unwavering commitment to others, guided by his deep devotion to God and the Immaculate Virgin Mary.

From his humble beginnings in Zduńska Wola to his intellectual pursuits in Rome, Kolbe embodied a relentless pursuit of truth and goodness. He sought not only to deepen his own faith but also to inspire others to find meaning and hope in their lives. His founding of the *Militia Immaculatae,* the *Knight of the Immaculate magazine*, and the creation of Niepokalanów stand as monumental achievements, each motivated by his desire to bring others closer to God.

But perhaps the greatest lesson Kolbe offers is the power of self-sacrifice. His decision to volunteer his life for Franciszek Gajowniczek in Auschwitz is a singular act of love that echoes through history. In that moment, Kolbe embodied Christ's teaching: "Greater love has no one than this, that someone lay down his life for his friends" (John 15:13).

Kolbe's sacrifice teaches us that true love is not transactional but unconditional. It is a love that seeks not to gain but to give, not to dominate but to serve. It is a love that transcends fear, hatred, and even death.

Kolbe's Relevance in Today's World

The challenges Kolbe faced—oppression, dehumanization, and the spread of hate—are not confined to his time. In many ways, the world today mirrors the struggles of Kolbe's era. Acts of bigotry, the marginalization of vulnerable groups, and the prevalence of violence and division remind us that the battle against evil is ongoing.

Kolbe's response to these challenges was rooted in his faith and belief in the inherent dignity of every person. He refused to meet hatred with hatred, choosing instead to respond with compassion and courage.

In Auschwitz, even as his body was subjected to the most brutal conditions, his spirit remained unbroken. His prayers, hymns, and words of encouragement brought light to one of the darkest places in human history.

For those navigating the complexities of modern life, Kolbe's example offers a roadmap for resistance against apathy and indifference. His actions challenge us to confront the injustices of our time—not with anger or despair, but with a commitment to truth and love.

A Call to Selflessness

Kolbe's life is a call to selflessness in a world increasingly driven by self-interest. His choice to give his life for another challenges us to rethink what it means to live fully. For Kolbe, life was not about personal achievement or comfort; it was about fulfilling God's will and serving others.

This selflessness can be emulated in our everyday lives. While few are called to the ultimate sacrifice Kolbe made, everyone has the opportunity to practice self-giving love. Small acts of kindness, the willingness to forgive, and the courage to stand up for what is right all reflect the spirit of Kolbe's legacy.

Kolbe reminds us that selflessness is not a weakness but a profound strength. It is a strength that builds communities, heals wounds, and fosters hope.

Faith as a Catalyst for Change

Kolbe's life underscores the transformative power of faith. His unwavering trust in God gave him the courage to face unimaginable suffering with peace and dignity. For Kolbe, faith was not a passive belief but an active force that shaped his thoughts, actions, and relationships.

In a world where faith is often dismissed as irrelevant or outdated, Kolbe's story challenges us to rediscover its power. His life demonstrates that faith is not an escape from reality but a lens through which to see it more clearly. It is a source of strength in times of weakness, a beacon of hope in times of despair, and a foundation for love in times of hate.

Kolbe's integration of faith with reason also offers a vital lesson for contemporary society. He believed that faith and intellectual inquiry were not in conflict but complementary. This approach can inspire modern believers to engage with the world's complexities without compromising their spiritual values.

Defying Hate with Love

Kolbe's ultimate legacy is his ability to defy hate with love. In a culture that often glorifies power and retribution, Kolbe's life reminds us of the redemptive power of forgiveness and compassion.

His actions in Auschwitz were a profound rejection of the Nazi ideology of hatred and dehumanization. By choosing to sacrifice his life for another, Kolbe declared the inviolable worth of every human being. His example compels us to confront hatred in all its forms, whether in our personal relationships or in the broader social and political landscape.

Kolbe's response to hatred was not passive acceptance but active love. This love was not limited to grand gestures; it was evident in his daily interactions, his prayers, and his commitment to uplifting others. His life challenges us to practice this kind of love in our own lives, even when it is difficult or costly.

A Legacy of Hope and Action

Kolbe's story does not end with his death. His canonization as a "Martyr of Charity" by Pope John Paul II, his recognition as a patron saint of various causes, and the countless lives he has inspired are a testament to the enduring impact of his life.

Today, Kolbe's example continues to resonate with those seeking to make a difference in the world. His influence can be seen in pro-life advocacy, addiction recovery programs, and movements promoting peace and reconciliation. His writings, prayers, and teachings offer spiritual nourishment for those striving to live lives of faith and love.

But Kolbe's legacy is not merely for saints or heroes; it is for everyone. His life invites us to reflect on how we can embody his values in our own unique circumstances.

A Call to Action

As we conclude this biography, the question arises: How can we live the Kolbe legacy in our own lives?

Kolbe's life teaches us that love is the most powerful force in the world. It is a force that can heal wounds, bridge divides, and transform darkness into light. By practicing selflessness, embracing faith, and choosing love over hate, we can honor Kolbe's memory and continue his mission.

In a world that often seems consumed by hatred and despair, Kolbe's story reminds us that every act of love, no matter how small, has the power to make a difference.

His life challenges us to be beacons of hope, agents of change, and witnesses to the transformative power of love.

Saint Maximilian Kolbe's life is a testament to the enduring power of faith, the unyielding strength of love, and the boundless potential of the human spirit. May his example inspire us to live lives of courage, compassion, and selflessness, defying hate with love in our own time and place.

A Final Reflection

Maximilian Kolbe's legacy is not confined to the past; it is a living call to action for each of us. As we navigate the challenges of our modern world, may we draw strength from his example and strive to embody his values in our own lives.

In the words of Kolbe himself: "Only love creates."

Let us create a world that reflects this truth—a world where love triumphs over hate, hope over despair, and faith over fear. In doing so, we carry forward the legacy of Saint Maximilian Kolbe, ensuring that his light continues to shine for generations to come.

Appendices

Timeline of Saint Maximilian Kolbe's Life

A chronological overview of significant events in Kolbe's life:

1894: Born as Rajmund Kolbe in Zduńska Wola, Poland.

1906: Receives a vision of the Virgin Mary offering him two crowns.

1910: Joins the Conventual Franciscans.

1912: Travels to Rome to study theology and philosophy.

1917: Founds the *Militia Immaculatae*.

1922: Begins publishing the *Knight of the Immaculate* magazine.

1927: Establishes Niepokalanów ("City of the Immaculate").

1930: Travels to Japan to establish a Marian center in Nagasaki.

1936: Returns to Poland due to health issues.

1939: Nazi Germany invades Poland; Kolbe shelters refugees, including Jews, at Niepokalanów.

1941: Arrested by the Gestapo and sent to Auschwitz; volunteers to die in place of Franciszek Gajowniczek.

August 14, 1941: Dies by lethal injection in the starvation bunker.

1982: Canonized as a "Martyr of Charity" by Pope John Paul II.

Selected Writings of Saint Maximilian Kolbe

A curated selection of Kolbe's most impactful writings to give readers direct insight into his thoughts and teachings:

On Marian Devotion:
"Never be afraid of loving the Blessed Virgin too much. You can never love her more than Jesus did."

On Sacrificial Love:
"Let us remember that love lives through sacrifice and is nourished by giving. Without sacrifice, there is no love."

On Hope in Suffering:
"For Jesus Christ, I am prepared to suffer still more."

On Faith and Science:
"Science, when properly understood, does not contradict faith but enhances it. Both are paths to understanding truth."

Prayers Inspired by Saint Maximilian Kolbe

A Prayer for Courage and Love

"O Lord, through the intercession of Saint Maximilian Kolbe, grant me the courage to love selflessly and the strength to face trials with unwavering faith. May I, like him, be a beacon of hope to those in need. Amen."

A Prayer for Marian Devotion

"Immaculate Virgin Mary, guide me as you guided Saint Maximilian Kolbe. Help me to serve others with love, humility, and devotion, always reflecting your light to the world. Amen."

A Prayer for Perseverance in Faith

"Saint Maximilian Kolbe, pray for me to remain steadfast in my faith, even in moments of doubt and difficulty. May I find strength in your example of sacrifice and unshakable trust in God. Amen."

References

Primary Sources

Kolbe's Writings:
- Kolbe, Maximilian. *Collected Writings of St. Maximilian Kolbe*. Missionaries of the Immaculata.

Papal Declarations:
- John Paul II, *Homily at the Canonization of St. Maximilian Kolbe*, October 10, 1982.

Biographies and Scholarly Works

Frossard, André. *Forget Not Love: The Passion of Maximilian Kolbe.* Ignatius Press, 1987.

Gajowniczek, Franciszek. *He Saved My Life: Reflections on St. Maximilian Kolbe.* Pauline Books, 1995.

Doino, William. *Saints and Sinners: Kolbe's Life and Legacy.* Catholic Historical Review, 2010.

Historical Context

Gilbert, Martin. *The Holocaust: A History of the Jews of Europe During the Second World War.* Henry Holt, 1985.

Cywinski, Piotr. *Auschwitz: A Monograph of the Martyrdom of Saints.* Auschwitz-Birkenau Memorial and Museum, 2015.

Documentaries

Maximilian: Saint of Auschwitz. Directed by Tony Haines, 2016.

Love and Sacrifice: The Life of Maximilian Kolbe. EWTN, 2018.

Printed in Dunstable, United Kingdom